All THINGS SQUIRRELS For Kids

FILLED WITH PLENTY OF FACTS, PHOTOS, AND FUN TO LEARN ALL ABOUT SQUIRRELS

ANIMAL READS

WWW.ANIMALREADS.COM

WHAT'S HIDING IN THE TREES?

The Secret Life of Squirrels 1
   Meet Nature's Acrobats!

Squirrel Basics: 5
   What Are These Furry Critters?

What Makes a Squirrel So Squirrelly? 9
   Features & Characteristics

The Squirrel Squad — 23
   Different Squirrel Species

Tree Houses & Hideouts: 43
   Where Squirrels Call Home

Nuts About Food: 51
   What's on a Squirrel's Menu?

Super Squirrel Skills 59

Growing Up Squirrel: 67
   From Tiny to Terrific! (Squirrel Life Cycle)

A Squirrely Finale! 79

Thank You! 83

THE SECRET LIFE OF SQUIRRELS

MEET NATURE'S ACROBATS!

Ready to jump into a world of fluffy tails, tiny paws, and some seriously impressive stunts? Well, tighten those laces, brave explorer, because we're about to spring into the wild and wonderful world of squirrels!

You might be thinking, *"Squirrels? You mean those little guys darting around the yard? What's so special about them?"* Yep, those speedy backyard visitors! Trust us, there's nothing ordinary about these seriously cool critters. Squirrels are astonishing acrobats, architects, and even professional tree-planters. And that's just the beginning.

Did you know?

For example, that squirrels can sprint up to 20 miles — or 32 kilometers — an hour? That's much faster than people can ride a bicycle!

Curious to know more?

Then join us as we dive into a pile of crunchy autumn leaves and uncover everything there is to know about these fuzzy little pals. From their cozy treetop homes to secret underground hideaways, their surprising favorite snacks, and even their athletic abilities — *which are seriously next level.* Yep, squirrels have some wild tricks up their furry sleeves.

We'll meet all sorts of squirrels along our journey — some who soar through the sky and others who prefer to keep their paws firmly on the ground. Whether you're new to the squirrel squad or a long-time fan, this book's packed with fun facts just for you.

ALL THINGS SQUIRRELS FOR KIDS | 3

So, hold on to your acorns because this is going to be

a nutty adventure!

SQUIRREL BASICS:
WHAT ARE THESE FURRY CRITTERS?

Squirrels are tiny creatures that live in gardens, parks, and forests. To better understand them, let's look at their **scientific classification**, which is how scientists organize all living things. It's similar to organizing your toys into different categories: putting the cars into one container, building blocks into another, and the stuffed animals in another. *You classify your toys by similarities, the same way scientists classify animals by similarity.* It's a system that helps us understand how animals, plants, and even tiny creatures are related to each other.

Squirrels belong to a group called "**mammals**." Mammals are animals that have fur or hair, breathe air, and give birth to live babies instead of eggs, for example. *In case you haven't guessed it, you are also a mammal!*

Within the group of mammals, squirrels belong to a smaller group called "**rodents**," alongside hamsters, rats, and mice. Rodents are known for their sharp front teeth, which keep growing all the time. These teeth are called "**incisors**," and rodents use them to chew through hard nuts and wood. To ensure the teeth never dull or wear out, rodents' incisors just KEEP GROWING.

Can you imagine if your front teeth kept growing and growing and growing?! A little strange, right? Well, it would be pretty neat if you were a squirrel who loved gnawing away on hard nuts and wood.

Within the rodent family, squirrels belong to a super special family group called "**Sciuridae**" (sigh-YUR-ih-day). It might look like a tongue-twister, but once you break it down, it's fun to say! It's just a fancy name for the squirrel family, which also includes chipmunks, marmots, and prairie dogs. Most animals in this group have bushy tails, big eyes, and tiny fingers that help them hold things like nuts.

WHAT MAKES A SQUIRREL SO SQUIRRELLY?
FEATURES & CHARACTERISTICS

Let's discover all the fascinating features that make these furry friends such successful critters. You might be surprised to learn that these backyard neighbors are some of nature's most remarkable athletes and clever problem-solvers! From their super-sharp teeth to fantastic memory power, squirrels are full of incredible surprises. Get ready to look at these common backyard visitors in a whole new way!

FUR COAT

Squirrels come in a rainbow of colors! You might spot them in shades of brown, gray, red, or even shiny black. And if you're *really* lucky, you might even see a rare **albino** squirrel with a fluffy, all-white coat! Their soft fur keeps them cozy, helping them stay warm as they scamper around, even in the dead of winter.

Peek-a-boo! A rare albino squirrel says hello!

Fun Fact:

Albino animals are like nature's rare snowflakes! They're born with white fur, feathers, or scales because their bodies don't make a chemical called **melanin**, which creates color. Instead of the usual dark eyes, albino animals often have pink or light blue eyes. You might spot an albino squirrel, peacock, or even a turtle — each is super special! And guess what? Humans can be albino, too! People with albinism often have light or white hair, very pale skin, and blue or pinkish eyes. They are also nature's super rare snowflake and absolutely beautiful in their own way!

Aside from their array of colors, squirrels also come in all sorts of sizes. The tiniest are the African pygmy squirrels, which are only about 4 inches long — just like a lemon! But then there's the fantastic Malabar giant squirrel, which can grow almost 3 feet (or 90 centimeters) long, including its tail. That's as big as a 3 to 4-year-old child! *Can you imagine that giant squirrel climbing up a tree in your backyard? What a sight that would be!*

TEETH

As you've learned in the previous chapter, squirrels have special front teeth called incisors. Since squirrels always gnaw on hard food like nuts and seeds, their teeth wear down quickly. **Nature to the rescue!** The more a squirrel chews on hard stuff and wears down its teeth, the more the teeth grow to replace what's been worn away. If a squirrel ever stopped snacking, their teeth could grow way too long and get super uncomfortable. But don't worry — squirrels are always on the lookout

ALL THINGS SQUIRRELS FOR KIDS 13

for tasty treats to munch. They've got no plans to stop crunching anytime soon!

Since squirrels constantly chew on stuff, their teeth are also very sharp. This comes in handy when cracking open an acorn or nibbling through some delicious pinecone seeds.

FLUFFY TAILS

A squirrel's fluffy tail is probably their most adorable feature. *Because is there anything cuter than a squirrel flicking its fluffy tail?* Lovable as they may

be, squirrel tails aren't just there for cuteness — they play an important role in their lives.

A squirrel's tail helps it **balance** when leaping from tree to tree. Sometimes, they even use their tail as an umbrella during rain to **keep dry** and **warm** when it gets too cold. *That's right, squirrels can use their fluffy tail as a blanket when the night is chilly!*

Lastly, squirrels also use their tails to **communicate** with one another. When they're happy or excited, they twitch their tails quickly. They flick their

tails slowly if they're feeling a little cautious or worried. Just like with a dog, if you want to know what a squirrel is feeling, pay attention to its tail!

Fun Fact:

Squirrels have a complex language. Not only do they use their tails to communicate, but they also "talk" to each other with squeals, barks, and clicks.

SQUIRREL SHENANIGANS! (BEHAVIOR)

If you've ever watched a squirrel, even for a few moments, you know they are active, lively, and *always on the go*. Indeed, most of the day for a squirrel is spent **foraging**. Foraging is what squirrels do to find food, and *they are experts at it!*

Squirrels use their fantastic sense of smell and keen eyesight to search for nuts, seeds, and fruits. They hop and scamper around and are always looking for a tasty treat. But squirrels aren't just looking

for their next meal. They know nuts and seeds don't grow year-round, so they must plan. Aside from foraging for food to eat *right now*, squirrels must also forage for the winter, when food is hard to find. Once they find food, squirrels bury their treasure trove of nuts and acorns all over the place to store them for later. This is called **caching**.

This little grey squirrel is planting snacks for later!

Fun fact:

Squirrels hide countless caches of food all over the place. They remember most of the places...but not all!

Squirrels have a fantastic sense of smell, so even if they forget where they buried their treasure, they can usually sniff it out later. But sometimes, they don't find their snacks soon enough, and those seeds grow into new trees. In this way, squirrels are nature's very own little tree-planters and gardeners!

While some animals like bears **hibernate** — *this is what it's called when an animal sleeps throughout the winter* — squirrels only slow down and get into a state called **torpor** — which is more like being sleepy rather than fully asleep. A squirrel can go

days and weeks without eating or drinking during torpor. They enjoy restful sleep in their cozy nests or burrows, but unlike bears, they can wake up, stretch, and eat from their buried cache treasure.

Fun Fact:

Animals that hibernate in the winter must eat a lot beforehand, so they put on extra fat. During their long winter sleep, their bodies use the extra fat so the animal stays alive, even if it does not eat. Bears, hedgehogs,

and bats are among the animals that hibernate. On the other hand, animals in torpor simply enjoy longer daytime sleep, so they need less energy but cannot store a lot of extra energy. They still need to wake up and go out looking for food. Squirrels, hedgehogs, and snakes are some of the animals that go into this state of torpor.

WHY IS IT A BAD IDEA TO WORK FOR SQUIRRELS?

They pay peanuts!

THE SQUIRREL SQUAD —

DIFFERENT SQUIRREL SPECIES

Squirrels survive and flourish in nearly every corner of the globe. No matter where you go, there's a chance you'll spot one of these energetic creatures skittering around. Next time you see a squirrel, take a moment to appreciate that **more than 200 squirrel species** are out there!

Let's get to know some of the most interesting!

EASTERN GRAY SQUIRREL

The Eastern gray squirrel is a widespread species found in North America. You might even spot one right outside your window or at the park! They typically measure around 17 to 20 inches in length, including their tail — or 43-50 centimeters — roughly the height of a small puppy. Fully grown, they can weigh up to 1.3 pounds, or half a kilogram — which is also the weight of a tiny puppy!

As you might guess from its name, the Eastern gray squirrel has **gray fur** of differing shades — some are darker and others relatively light. This species has a white belly and a large bushy tail that it swishes around when excited or scared.

When making a home, Eastern gray squirrels are experts at building **dreys** — that's what we call squirrels' nests or homes. They love creating their dreys in the forks of tree branches, using leaves, twigs, and even bits of fur or feathers.

Fun Fact:

Animal fur makes excellent insulation for nests, keeping squirrels super warm in winter. The sneaky but friendly builders will try to steal fur from wild animals like deer or rabbits but will also befriend a pet dog or cat so they can steal their fur. They're furry little fur thieves!

Eastern gray squirrels are pretty social animals. They live in loose groups and even play with each other. But sometimes, if the group gets too big or crowded, they can become aggressive toward one another. But overall, Eastern gray squirrels are lively and harmless inhabitants of yards, parks, and woods.

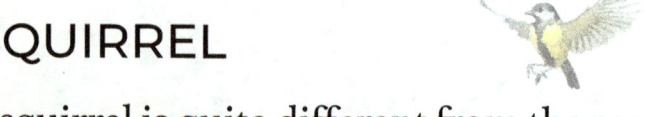

Next time you go for a walk in the woods, look up and keep your eyes peeled near the tree tops for a squirrel nest. They like to build their nests high because it keeps them safe from predators.

FOX SQUIRREL

The fox squirrel is quite different from the squirrels you might see every day! These unique squirrels are **larger than most**, weighing up to 3 pounds or 1.4 kilograms. That may not sound huge, but it

makes them the biggest tree squirrels in North America! They can grow between 18 to 27 inches long (45-65 centimeters), including their bushy tails. That's about the **average size of a cat!**

Fox squirrels can be found in all kinds of places, from quiet forests to busy city parks. They've become great at living alongside people, often making their homes in old trees or even in attics (*like your grandma's!*) But their favorite homes are in open woodlands where they can roam freely without too much underbrush. Isn't that cool?

Fox squirrels come in shades of brown or gray with hints of orange. Some even have **beautiful reddish fur**, just like a fox! These squirrels tend to stay on the ground much more than most other

squirrel species. Yet, although they are heavier than most other species, they are still brilliant tree climbers.

Fox squirrels are sometimes confused with other species, such as red or gray squirrels. But if you are in doubt, just look at their size. If it's the biggest squirrel you've ever seen, it might be a fox squirrel!

Fun Fact:

Fox squirrels get their name from their incredible resemblance to foxes, not only because of their red fur but also because of their impressive size.

Freeze! This speedy red squirrel is ready for its photoshoot...

RED SQUIRREL

Red squirrels are known for their **reddish-orange fur** and fluffy tails. They are found foraging for yummy treats in Europe, Asia, and a few places in North America.

The red squirrel is a charming and feisty little creature with tufted hair on its ears, which makes them appear extra-large and pointy. They typically

measure around 13 to 18 inches (33-45 centimeters), **smaller than the other squirrels** we have learned about. They have a max weight of 1 lb. 12 oz, which is only 800 grams!

    These squirrels build their nests high up in trees using twigs, leaves, and soft materials like moss. This keeps them warm and safe from the reach of predators. Plus, it makes a nice spot to nap after a long day of tree-hopping and acorn-collecting.

Fun Fact:

Nests and dreys are practically identical words, except nests are used for every animal that builds a home, and dreys are used only to mean squirrel nests.

Red squirrels are agile and full of energy. They gracefully run, leap, and climb trees, making them fun to watch! But they can be shy too — if you want to observe them, be quiet and respectful of their space. If you aren't sure you're looking at a red squirrel, just watch for their tufted ears. This **unique** feature isn't common. So, if it has very **pointy ears**, it's probably a red squirrel.

This red squirrel is leaping into action!

Super Fun Fact:

Squirrels are extraordinary jumpers and can leap a distance that's over 10 times their body length. This is like you being able to jump over an SUV in one hop!

FLYING SQUIRREL

As you might have guessed by their name, flying squirrels can fly, although not exactly the way you might imagine. These amazing creatures don't actually fly like birds. Instead, they **glide** through the air using a unique skin flap that stretches from their wrists to their ankles, called a **patagium**. *A patagium is like a cape attached to your wrists and ankles. Spread your arms and legs wide open, and BAM! The cape stretches out and forms a big square.* That's what happens when flying squirrels glide in the air. Their patagium stretches from wrist to ankle, and when

they jump and spread their arms and legs, they glide through the air like a real-life superhero!

In North America, there are two primary species of flying squirrels: the Northern flying squirrel and the Southern flying squirrel. The Northern flying squirrel is slightly larger and can live happily in colder climates, often found in fir-tree forests that offer a rich diet of fungus and lichen. On the other end, its Southern sibling is a bit smaller and prefers mixed forests, where it can indulge in an abundance of nuts and fruits.

Did you know that flying squirrels are **nocturnal**? That means they sleep during the day and are active at night. Their big, round eyes help them see better in the dark. While exploring the nighttime forest, these squirrels leap between trees and glide across the night sky in search of food.

Flying squirrels are also excellent neighbors to other animals. They often share tree holes with other squirrels to keep warm during the cold winter nights. *How cozy and friendly is that?*

MALABAR GIANT SQUIRREL

These magnificent creatures are not your regular backyard squirrels! Oh no, these are creatures that really live up to their name.

The Malabar giant squirrel is also known as the Indian giant squirrel, a large, tree-dwelling squirrel that lives in the tropical forests of India. They're called **giant** for a reason — these incredible animals can grow up to 44 inches long (just over 1 meter), almost as long as a baseball bat! Half their length is comprised of their long, beautiful, bushy

tail. These giant squirrels also weigh a lot — on average, they weigh in at around 3.5 pounds (1.5 kilograms), but they can reach weights of 6.6 pounds (3 kilograms), about the size of a newborn baby human or a small dog!

One of the most extraordinary things about these squirrels is their **colorful fur.** Malabar Giant Squirrels have brown, beige, orange, and even purple fur patches! This helps them blend into the tropical trees and stay hidden from predators. In fact, unlike other types of squirrels, these giant guys don't typically run from predators at all. If frightened, they often flatten themselves against the tree trunk and camouflage themselves to avoid danger!

No worries, just chillin'!

Given their size and weight, these squirrels can't fly or glide like the flying squirrels we just learned about, but they still have some impressive jumping abilities. The Malabar giant squirrel can leap a great distance from tree to tree — up to 20 feet or 6 meters!

These squirrels prefer to live alone and love to live high up in the trees, where it's hard for anyone to bother them. They eat fruits, flowers, nuts, and bird eggs. They are most active in the first and last part of the day and rest when the sun is highest (and hottest). Thankfully, the fantastic Malabar giant squirrel is plentiful and not at risk of extinction. If you live in India or travel there, maybe you'll see one someday!

PYGMY SQUIRREL

From one of the biggest squirrels in the world, now let's meet the teeny tiniest. **The mighty pygmy squirrel!**

These little creatures are *so* small they can fit in the palm of your hand. Most pygmy squirrels are only about 5 inches long (about 12 centimeters) from their nose to the tip of their tail. When we say

tiny, we mean it. These micro-squirrels only weigh under one ounce (25 grams) or about the same weight as a single slice of bread.

Pygmy squirrels live in Africa, Asia, and South America, with different kinds (**breeds**) living in different parts of the world. Some of the most common breeds are the plain pygmy squirrel from Southeast Asia and the African pygmy squirrel found in the tropical rainforests of Central Africa.

Pygmy squirrels come in many colors, including brown, black, and gray. As you might imagine, a pygmy squirrel's small size means it's uber-packed with energy and very fast. They zip around branches, looking for tasty things like seeds, insects, and fruit.

Next time you hold a piece of bread, close your eyes. Can you imagine having a tiny pygmy squirrel in your hand? That is exactly how heavy it would feel! Except, of course, a pygmy squirrel would be furry and probably too busy to sit still for long!

WHAT DID THE TREE SAY TO THE SQUIRREL?

Leaf me alone!

TREE HOUSES & HIDEOUTS:
WHERE SQUIRRELS CALL HOME

Adaptable, clever, resourceful, and ever-so-adorable, squirrels live on every continent except Antarctica and Australia. Isn't it strange that Australians don't have squirrels scampering all over?!

Fun Fact:

While Australia was never home to squirrel species, people have introduced a few Eastern gray squirrels. There aren't many, and the few that have survived are considered pests because they compete with Australian wildlife, like possums, for food and habitat.

To those who live on other continents, however, squirrels are a common sight. We're sure you've seen squirrels climbing trees, looking for nuts at the park, or running across your backyard.

Many species of squirrels love to live **high up in the trees.** Tree squirrels make their nests high in the branches to quickly escape from predators chasing them on the ground.

Fun Fact:

Squirrels can turn their ankles 180 degrees, which means their feet can turn backward! This allows them to sprint down trees, head first, as fast as they sprint up them.

The squirrel nest looks like a big ball; as we know, it is made of twigs, leaves, fur, and moss. Inside is a hollow space about the size of a soccer ball: this is where the squirrel sleeps and stays safe from the weather and other animals. Although squirrel nests are up on trees all year round, they are easier to spot in winter when the trees are mostly bare and don't have many leaves left.

Want to hear something truly fun?

Some tree squirrels make more than one nest. They make a "main" one and then a backup one if they are forced to move.

Other squirrels prefer to live closer to the ground, so they are called ground squirrels. Rather than building nests, they dig **burrows**, like underground tunnels, where they sleep and hide their winter food. *Imagine having a secret tunnel network where you could zip around unseen and hide all your candy — wouldn't that be cool? That's precisely what these squirrels have!*

So, we know that tree squirrels build nests on trees, and ground squirrels dig burrows underground. Want to guess where flying squirrels live?

Like tree squirrels, flying squirrels spend most of their time on trees. But instead of building dreys,

Here's a family of ground squirrels peeking out of their burrow!

flying squirrels find **holes in tree trunks** to use for their homes. Finding a cool hole and decorating it with moss or twigs gives these flighty squirrels a safe and warm place to hide during the day. This is important because they mainly come out at night.

But that's not all the places squirrels can build a home. Some squirrels even live in people's attics!

Quite a few animals have adapted to city life, including raccoons and coyotes. Yet the squirrel is

probably the most welcomed out of those! Now, as lovely as an attic may be, there are certainly better places for squirrels to live. It's best to let wildlife live in their natural homes and discourage them from living too close to us whenever possible.

This little guy is gathering materials for his drey!

WHAT DO RICH SQUIRRELS EAT?

CASH-ews!

NUTS ABOUT FOOD:
WHAT'S ON A SQUIRREL'S MENU?

These marvelous critters are **omnivores**, which means they eat both plants and animals — *kind of like us humans do!* Their favorite foods are seeds, nuts, and fruits, but they also munch on insects and sometimes even snack on bird eggs. To find all this food, squirrels spend their days **foraging** - that's the fancy word for searching and gathering food. Think of it as going on a treasure hunt for breakfast, lunch, and dinner!

Squirrels are among the best food finders on the planet. They've developed amazing skills that help them spot food from far away, create clever hiding spots for their treasures, and remember where they've hidden most of their snacks. These special abilities have helped squirrels become successful survivors all around the world!

But what do they like to eat?

You probably already know that squirrels are nuts about nuts! And yes, they go crazy for all things nuts, such as acorns, walnuts, and pine nuts. Squirrels love to bury their nuts for later, but not all in the same place, of course! To ensure that most of their hoard remains secret, squirrels use many different hiding spots — hiding one nut here and another there. This strategy is called "**scatter-hoarding**," and it is super smart indeed.

If another animal discovers one of their hidden food stashes, they don't lose *all* their food, just a ti-

ny part. Plus, it also means they have food available in lots of different places. We know that, sometimes, a forgetful squirrel might not remember a particular spot, but never mind — a new oak tree will grow there instead! In the world of squirrels, nothing ever goes to waste.

Aside from nuts, squirrels also enjoy eating seeds. Sunflower seeds, pumpkin seeds — you name it, they'll eat it! Squirrels are also huge fans of fruits and veggies. They enjoy apples, berries, carrots, and peas. They're not picky eaters at all and love their healthy diet! Some squirrels will even eat insects and small birds' eggs when they can find them.

Another interesting thing about a squirrel's diet is that their eating habits change with the seasons. When the weather is warm, and fruits are abundant, squirrels happily feast on all sorts of berries and other juicy treats. Yet when winter rolls around and fruits dry up, most of their diet comprises acorns, nuts, and seeds. This means that squirrels also help maintain the balance of the plants in their ecosystem. In their own cute way, they help our forests and gardens grow! It's incredible how even tiny creatures can greatly impact the world around us.

Now, here's one thing we mentioned briefly: squirrels are also sneaky thieves. *Have you ever put out bird food only to see it robbed by a neighborhood squirrel?* Squirrels will go through a lot of trouble to score a super tasty meal, and if we make it so easy for them, they are happy!

Still, it's essential to let squirrels find their own food. If they get used to being fed all the time by

Hmmm... I'm pretty sure this was meant for me!

humans, they might lose the ability to forage. If we give them leftover human food to eat, we might even make them ill. That would be terrible!

As cute and friendly as squirrels may be, it's important to remember that they are capable and primarily wild animals. Let the wild be wild — admire them, but please don't feed them!

SUPER SQUIRREL SKILLS

Squirrels are fascinating creatures with incredible acrobatic abilities! Let's explore some of the skills that make these fluffy-tailed gymnasts so unique.

CLIMBING & JUMPING GYMNASTS

As you already know, squirrels are expert climbers, and they can jump impressively far. Squirrels have very **powerful legs** (which help them jump), **sharp claws**, and **flexible toes** (which help them grab onto tree branches.) Their claws, which are really like built-in climbing shoes, also help them climb trees quickly. Squirrels scurry up and down trees faster than most people can run on flat ground!

Of course, all this is added to their ability to **turn their ankles the opposite way around**, as we learned earlier. There truly is no end to a squirrel's acrobatic tree-climbing skills, that's for sure!

CHEEKY STORAGE UNITS

With all that running, jumping, and landing, you might be wondering how on earth a squirrel can also carry nuts and seeds. Since squirrels don't wear backpacks, they must have a way of stashing their goodies, right? And they do. **They carry food in their cheeks!**

Squirrels have special pouches inside their cheeks that can stretch and expand. This allows them to stuff a whole lot of nuts, seeds, and acorns inside. *It's like a built-in, expandable grocery bag!* They use their paws and claws to grab food and stuff it into their cheek pouches, much like a hamster does.

Once they have their cheeks full of treats, squirrels look for a clever spot to store their food. Usually, they will look for holes in trees, but sometimes, they dig a hole and bury their yummy treasures. They must be sneaky and hide their stash well; otherwise, they risk it being found by other animals.

Squirrels return to their hiding spots to dig out their food days, weeks, and even months after they have hidden them. A single squirrel can select thousands of spots over just a single season.

Would you remember where you left all your toys if you had hidden them all in different spots a few months ago? We definitely don't think we could!

I remember burying something riiiight around here!

HOW SQUIRRELS ADAPT TO CHANGING SEASONS

As the seasons change, so do the needs of squirrels. In winter, when food is scarce, squirrels rely on their superb memory to find the food they hid

during the fall. If you have ever seen a squirrel digging in the dirt, it was likely searching for its secret stash.

Winter also brings chilly temperatures, but don't worry, squirrels are prepared. Their fur thickens so they can stay extra warm, and it fluffs up to offer even better insulation. If you have ever lived with a fluffy dog, you might already know about winter and summer fur changes.

Flying squirrels use an extra tactic to keep warm in winter — they work and live in groups, sharing nests and cuddles to combine their body heat for additional warmth. *Pretty clever, right?*

When spring arrives, squirrels adapt to the warmer weather by shedding thick winter fur. Imagine how excited they must be to see all the new buds and fresh leaves growing! After only eating stored nuts and seeds in winter, they probably look forward to some new tasty fresh treats! Many squirrel species also enjoy the return of insects and bird eggs added to their diet.

Summer is a bustling time for squirrels — it is their busiest season. They can enjoy a greater diet

with more fresh food, and they also have to forage and store treats for the upcoming winter. Summer is also when baby squirrels are born, so the parents must find enough food to feed their entire family.

Speaking of families, let's learn where baby squirrels come from.

GROWING UP SQUIRREL:

FROM TINY TO TERRIFIC! (SQUIRREL LIFE CYCLE)

Like us, squirrels go through all sorts of different stages as they grow from babies to senior squirrels. As squirrels go through each step, they learn new lessons that help them become better at surviving and thriving in the wild. Let's explore each life stage of these fantastic creatures.

SQUIRREL PUPS

Baby squirrels are called **kits** or **pups**. When newborns, they are incredibly tiny, totally hairless, and their eyes and ears are closed — so they are deaf *and* blind. A newborn squirrel can be around 1 to 1.5 inches (3 centimeters) long, which is only about the length of a paperclip! They're also very light, weighing about as much as a couple of coins stacked together. Squirrels come into this big world as part of a **litter** of brothers and sisters — sometimes, as many as 7 or 8 can be born at the same time!

Here's a cozy litter snuggled up in their nest!

After birth, the baby squirrels live in a nursery within the nest their parents built high up in the trees or in a burrow. In the early days of their lives, the pups stay snuggled with their siblings in the drey while their mom goes out to find food for herself and her babies. Meanwhile, the dad squirrel helps guard the nest from creatures that might want to disturb their peaceful family life. He's the bodyguard of the nest!

The kits stay snuggled up in their nest for the first few weeks, drinking milk from their mom when she returns. During this nursery period, the baby squirrels grow quickly. They gradually develop fur, and their eyes and ears open. At around 5 to 6 weeks old, they start moving around more and even begin to nibble on solid foods their mom brings back for them.

SQUIRREL SCHOOL: YOUNG SQUIRRELS IN THE JUVENILE STAGE

Once kits grow a bit older, around 6 to 10 weeks old, they enter the **juvenile stage** — perhaps the matching stage you are in, as a human, right now! This is a very important time in squirrels' lives — they still need adults to guide and teach them, but they are starting their journey to independence. Primarily, they are learning to **wean** and **forage**.

Weaning is when an animal starts eating solid food and stops drinking its mother's milk and relying solely on her for food. Although human babies wean within months of birth, they still rely

on their parents for food — they still can't buy or cook food until they are much older!

The young squirrels must learn to forage on their own. Without this skill, they'll have a hard time surviving when they grow up. Squirrels learn by closely watching their parents and fellow squirrels. This helps them understand the ropes and discover the best foods to snack on. It's not always smooth sailing, though — young squirrels might take a few falls from branches or struggle to crack open those hard-to-get nuts. But with practice and determination, they eventually get the hang of it, proving they're ready for the big, exciting world!

ALMOST GROWN: THE ADOLESCENT STAGE

Young squirrels spend more time alone, away from their families during this stage. They are around 6 to 9 months old and ready for independent adventures. This is just like how we become more self-reliant as we grow up! Young squirrels start exploring the big world out there, learning all sorts of skills that will be essential for their adult lives. They practice finding their own food, climbing trees, and staying out of trouble with other critters.

Growing up means bigger jumps — Weeee!

As squirrels become more independent, they also start looking for a place to call their own. They do this by marking their territory. How do squirrels mark their territory, you wonder? They use their **scent glands**, which are located on their face and paws, to leave a smell that tells other squirrels, *"Hey, this is my cozy corner of the world!"*

Finding the perfect territory is essential for a young squirrel. It needs to be the right size for them to find

enough food and also provide safe places to hide from predators. This process can be challenging, but it's an essential part of growing up for our bushy-tailed buddies.

ALL GROWN UP: ADULTHOOD

Squirrels are typically considered adults when they reach one year of age. They leave their mom, find or build their own nests, and start gathering their own food. They're young adults now and can do everything big squirrels can do!

Once fully grown, squirrels spend most of their time looking for food and storing it away for later. As adult squirrels, they can now jump from branch to branch, run up and down trees super-fast, and remember (*almost*) all the places where they hid their food.

Adult squirrels will start thinking about starting a family and having their own babies at this stage. Female squirrels are pretty picky when it comes to choosing a partner. They want to make sure they find the perfect match!

So, what do they do? They test the boys out by playing a game of chase. It might look like a lot of fun, but this game helps the females figure out which male is the strongest, fastest, and smartest. The winner gets to be her partner, and they start a brand-new squirrel family together. Female squirrels usually have babies once or twice a year. When the kits are born, the whole cycle starts all over again.

Most squirrels live around 6 to 12 years in the wild. However, in captivity, squirrels have been known to make it to almost 20 years!

WHAT'S A SQUIRREL'S FAVORITE SUBJECT?

His-TREE!

A SQUIRRELY FINALE!

WHOA, we've learned a lot about squirrels, haven't we? We've traveled through the treetops, explored squirrel hideouts, and discovered the secrets of these furry acrobats.

The next time you spot a squirrel in your backyard or at the park, share some fun facts you've learned with your friends or family. And keep observing nature and enjoying the wonders around you. Who knows — maybe one day you'll discover something new about squirrels or even become a squirrel researcher yourself?!

Thank you for joining us on this wild journey through the world of squirrels. Stay curious, young animal lover, keep exploring, and never stop learning about the incredible creatures that share our planet.

STAY SQUIRRELLY, MY FRIENDS!

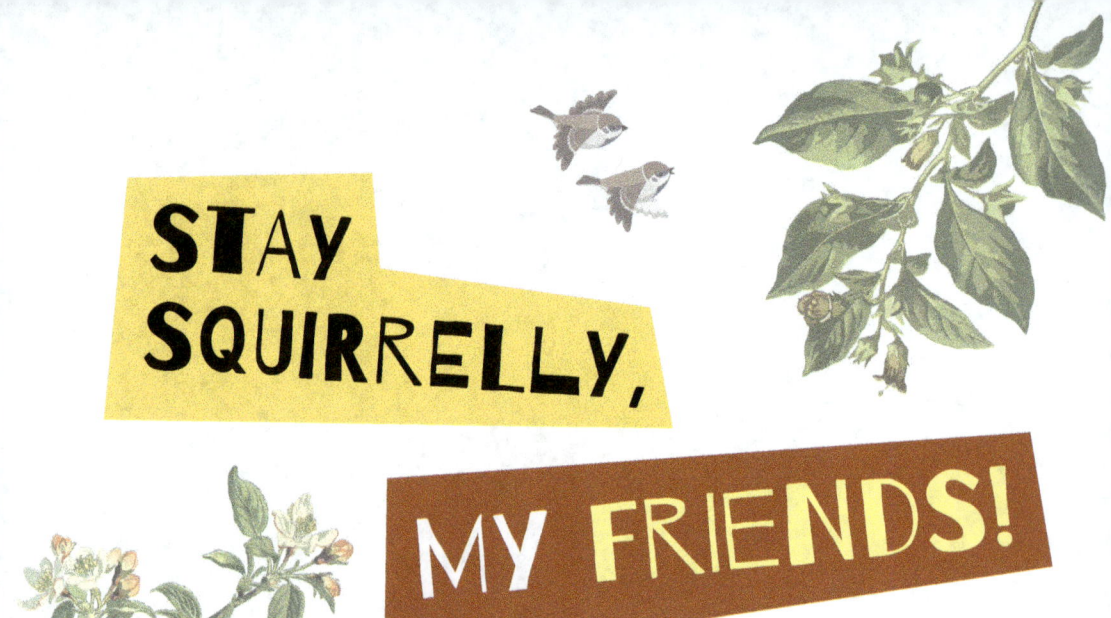

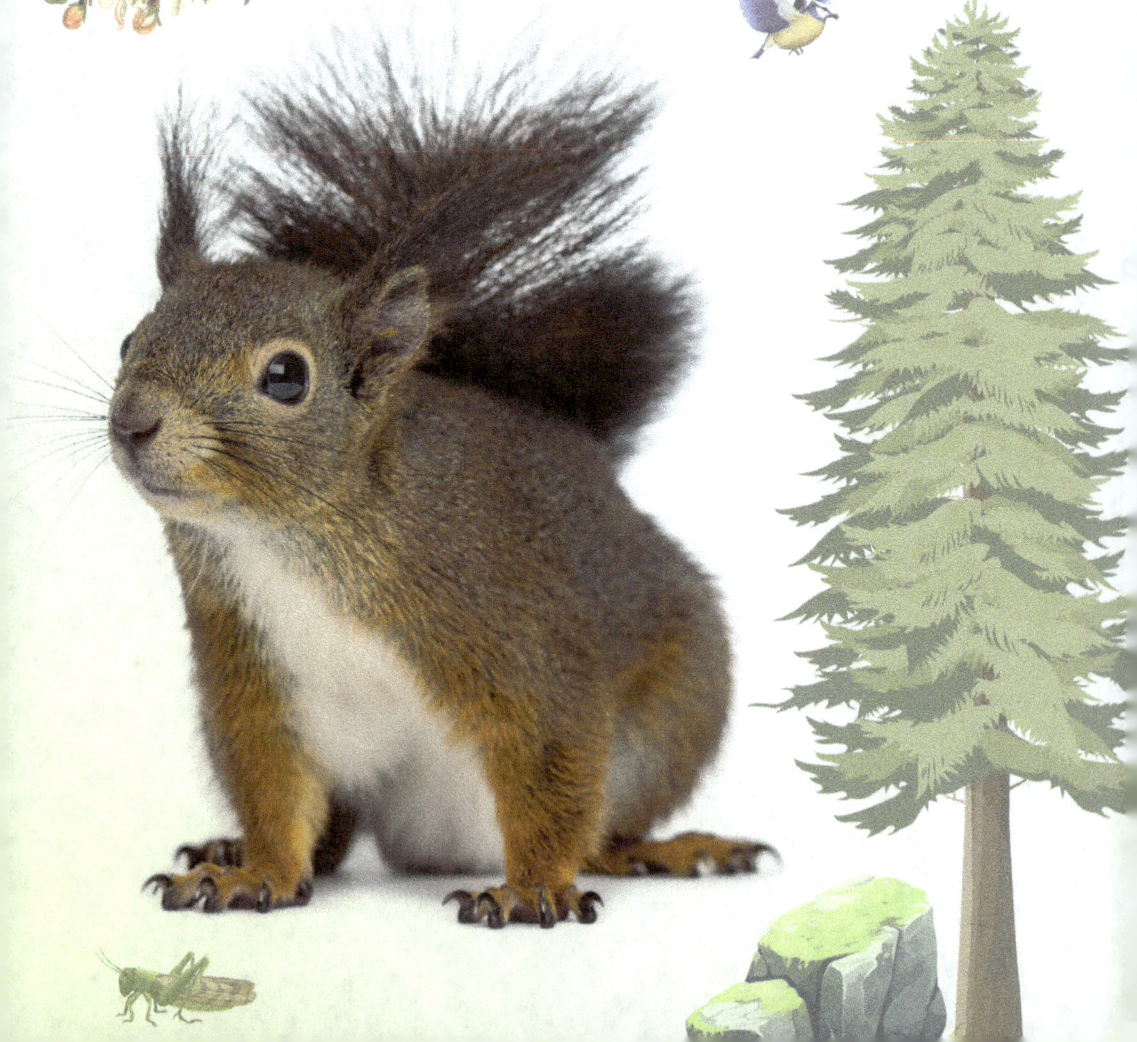

THANK YOU!

Thank you for reading this book and for allowing us to share our love for squirrels with you!

If you've enjoyed this book, please let us know by leaving a rating and a brief review wherever you made your purchase! This helps us spread the word to other readers!

Thank you for your time, and have an awesome day!

For more information, please visit:
www.animalreads.com

© Copyright 2025 — All rights reserved Admore Publishing

ISBN: 978-3-96772-182-9

ISBN: 978-3-96772-183-6

ISBN: 978-3-96772-184-3

Animal Reads at www.animalreads.com

The content contained within this book may not be reproduced, duplicated, or transmitted without direct written permission from the author or the publisher.

Under no circumstances will any blame or legal responsibility be held against the publisher or author for any damages, reparation, or monetary loss due to the information contained within this book. Either directly or indirectly.

Published by Admore Publishing: Gotenstraße, Berlin, Germany

www.admorepublishing.com

www.ingramcontent.com/pod-product-compliance
Lightning Source LLC
LaVergne TN
LVHW021340080526
838202LV00004B/246